HUMAN LOOKING

Also by Andy Jackson

Among The Regulars
The Thin Bridge
Immune Systems
Music Our Bodies Can't Hold

ANDY JACKSON

HUMAN LOOKING

NEW POEMS

First published 2021
from the Writing and Society Research Centre
at Western Sydney University
by the Giramondo Publishing Company
PO Box 752
Artarmon NSW 1570 Australia
www.giramondopublishing.com

Cover and design by Jenny Grigg
Typesetting by Andrew Davies
in 9/15 pt Tiempos Regular

Printed and bound by Ligare Book Printers
Distributed in Australia by NewSouth Books

A catalogue record for this
book is available from the
National Library of Australia.

ISBN: 978-1-925818-85-7

The Giramondo Publishing Company acknowledges the support of Western Sydney University in the implementation of its book publishing program.

This project has been assisted by the Commonwealth Government through the Australia Council, its arts funding and advisory body.

for Anne Mary Jackson (1940–2019)
and Norman Charles Jackson (1926–1973)

Contents

Opening

Opening

The incision – mine anyway –
begins below the back of the neck

and ends just above the coccyx.
Surgical stitches quietly dissolve,

leave a thick scar – a blurred, insistent line.
As each layer of skin dies, it whispers to the next

the form and story of the wound.
This is how I continue, intact.

Yet now, as I strain to lift this
too-heavy object, the long suture ruptures

in my head – the scar tearing open.
You might think this visceral confession

only an image of mine. But you are becoming
this unstitching, this sudden opening.

Operations

GP referral to specialist (24.5.1976)

this 5-year-old boy

I have been able to reassure his
mother about the former, but the latter is
worrying her, particularly as the father
as a result of severe

could you please outline his
future

letter from professor of paediatrics (17.9.1982)

we like to
feel quite certain
abnormality
the very characteristic
opinion

disorder of the connective
I think
suspect
mild or even serious
really serious problems

a little
bit of nuisance
this process should be repeated
allowed to progress to a severe stage
to give a very simple

and factual description
just a name
just what he feels
an error
cropping up

operation sheet (7.1.1987)

complicating through the old
incision down into
the possible
to expose the sacral
the fusion mass
wires sublaminar wires double wires
contoured rods into the wings
of the ilium
moderate correction but remarkable
how rigid the spine
stripped and decorticated and bone
graft laid out on the concave
wounds were all
closed this lad
has lost
a lot of blood

1590 mls he can be
mobilised when into a low
sort of brace satis
factory

nurse's progress sheet (8–15.1.1987)

tolerating   quiet   drain continues
as ordered   tolerating this   reasonably
unsettled   gauze   found at 8 a.m.
leaking   dressing   reinforced
some relief   light diet   not very
interested   bile stained   fluid no visitors
pressure care   morphine   a small bleed
quite settled   cooperative   from mid-back
sitting   on edge   unsupported
tends to lose   balance   looks pale still
slight   down   unsettled early in the
evening found half out of bed at 11.25 p.m. with his feet on the floor
awaiting signature   dis or iented   needs
encouragement   quiet and in   tact
obs stable   hair washed   brace re al
igned   and he stood up and walked

a few steps for discharge tomorrow home

letter from mother (23.1.1987)

dear

we hardly know

but

the extra

regular

trauma of a hospital stay

the whole person

in isolation

wonderful

operation

anxiety of the days

we couldn't have chosen

see you when we come back

Separation

A fly in the operating theatre
bothers the cameras.
Our two hearts beat in one sac,
against each other.   I feel

you, on the other trolley,
being pulled away from me.
A burning coldness at my side –
the space there, beating, boneless.

When I wake,   a nurse
and my father place a mirror
along the length of the bed.
You are just you now – you are one,

said like a chant or a mass.
But I know it is they who have made me.
And you're gone –   collapsed
lung, too many infections, the trauma

of separation. You are the price
of my existence from now on.
One has to do harm   to do good.
There are many more surgeries ahead.

~

I feel a breath at my neck
and expect you there –
but it's a hard wind, your absence

pushing at my bones
through an open window. Where
are you now? And that small voice

is only the radio I left on last night.
You are my wound, my pain.
I won't say *phantom*. I miss

the tenderness with which you'd
stroke and explore this skin
as if we were two. You

put words in my mouth and
calmed me with that voice.
Hold me again and forgive me

for letting them kill you,
those philosophers with scalpels.
They make a life *normal*

by breaking it in two.
In my passport, only one name.
I can almost see your head on my shoulder,

cut roughly out of the frame.
I'm still learning how to walk straight,
how to carry my weight without you.

Is that why they   still stare?
Can they sense   the vacuum at my side?
The wound is   weeping. I'm afraid

it may be infected.   Now,
all I want is sleep,   where you will
slide back into this   warm home

of flesh, our shared   dream.
I lie awake with   my shadow
and it doesn't –   or can't – move.

Venus with BIID

the surgeon gives me a story so
the nurses won't be suspicious
bandages the leg gives crutches
an accident happened while I
was overseas on my holiday is
what I'll tell them back home

I remember as a boy I watched
you pass in callipers   stiff-gait
clicking acutely focused private
you transfixed me I recognised
myself in your complete beauty
everyone else seemed ashamed

I've limped from room to room
in my home that stinks of tears
outside I hide this limb they
call healthy or tuck it under
my body for the cold relief of
numbness but feeling returns

so I'm here because pills god
meditation they're all useless
I learnt precisely where to aim
the gun to ensure the least pain
how to immerse a limb in dry
ice   but I've never had quite

I don't exp
ect you to
understand
most thin
k a broken
body is un

liveable m
y only dis
ability is t
hat I don't
have the o
ne I need

look clos
ely at a m
irror (ev
en yours)
smashed
any shard

can beco
me a scal
pel a key
to set yo
ur body
map free

enough courage or painkillers
caught myself staring at train-
tracks but I don't want to die

soon while I'm anaesthetised
he'll make a precise and deep
incision cauterise saw suture
I don't care what happens to it
now the leg has gone I'm whole

when we
lifted the
venus de
milo out
of her n
iche we
gasped at
her beauty

Unhomely

alternating lines with Randolph Bourne's essay 'The Handicapped' (1911)

he knows the atmosphere better than you do, so
        the doors of the deformed man are always locked
though from his lounge of shadows, a surprising view
        who has not all his treasures in the front window
whose facade deflects the usual questions

        extraordinarily sensitive to others' first impressions
a little distant, yet very much here
        inherited platitudes vanish at the first touch
of medical specialists or curious strangers
        if he can stand the first shock, he will want to burrow in

to cobble together some semblance of finesse
        he does not cry for the moon
only our detached aesthetics – he dreams of saying
        I solved my difficulties by evading them, the desperate step
out of the crawlspace of wounded knowledge towards

        a profound sympathy for all the ugly, queer and crotchety
this luminous splinter buried deep in the chest
        a lively interest in watching how people behave
his reticent mouth opening towards
        those few who by some secret sympathy will respond

their bodies, the shape of skeleton keys
        one only exists, so to speak, with friends

once all those useful tools are downed
    one's self-respect can begin to grow like a weed
        something unwanted that won't disappear

Borne away by distance

from the final chapter of Frankenstein *by Mary Shelley*

You may give up your purpose
but mine is assigned to me
I often thought
breathed
composing the burning of my own species
the task of my returning
exhausted
I, this wonderful catastrophe
the remains of words

gigantic in stature
distorted in proportions
this pause
turning toward
tremendous being

I attempt to speak but the words die away on my lips
at length I gather resolution
groans
of love and sympathy
throw a torch into a pile of buildings
and sit among the ruins

I hope to meet with
unfolding

believe the creature
sublime and transcendent

I am alone
you hate me
but cannot
equal my being
that which must be

ice raft   extremity   ashes   this frame
torn by extinction

I shall exult in flames
the winds
borne away by distance

Aesthetic surgery

Gloved and masked, he goes in through an incision at my navel,
so the scarring is minimal. The natural look is hard work.
He knows these decisions are emotional,
is first in the search results, so I trust him.
Sculpting a photo's not enough – flesh must be improved.

He knows scarring is emotional,
as a better shape is torn out of this deteriorating body.
We're all self-conscious about changes.
Sculpting a photo's not enough – flesh must be improved,
so I accept the loss of sensation, risk of complications, necrosis.

We're all self-conscious, being torn out of shape.
After the infection, I go to him again, hoping for different results.
Side-effects include an increased risk of self-harm,
loss of sensation, complications, necrosis. I accept
a discount for agreeing to the before and after shots.

He goes in again, hoping for different results,
more followers, more likes. Soon, I can move on –
my spirit lifted, watching from above.
A discount for agreeing to the before and after shots
is one way to help me forget the mortality rates, dream

of more followers, more likes, my spirit lifted.
He's first in the search results, so I trust him.

It's not insecurity beneath these stitches, but love,
a way to help me forget the mortality rates.
Gloved and masked, he goes in through an incision at my navel.

Pillow angel

Love signs the consent forms
in the presence of the specialists, who assure us
she will always have the mind of a toddler.

A black stork lands outside the kitchen window.

She can't talk, keep her head up, grip a toy or change
her sleeping position. She is fed with a tube.
We're careful who we tell about the treatment.

Some become flooded with silence and turn away.

Of all the procedures, what unsettles you most
is the oestrogen therapy to limit her growth.
Don't worry, none of this will happen to you.

In the Bible, an angel will appear in human form.

Metal and pulleys are nothing compared to human touch,
a parent lifting their own forever-small angel.
After the surgeries, it seemed her pain was minimal.

I look into her eyes and try my best to imagine.

She startles easily, loves classical music
and will never understand 'autonomy'.
If only we could live forever to care for her.

The black stork flies off. We can't be sure

she recognises us, but where we place her,
usually on a large pillow, she stays,
surrounded by soft toys.

Beauty, from the other side

Aged twelve, before surgery to fix the scoliosis, I formed
an idea a certain girl might like me. I found her beautiful.
Or was it just that I knew others did? I can't be sure.
I don't think we ever spoke. What I do remember
are the insults I absorbed like splinters, how my body
held and resisted them. Like nested dolls, each identity

contains within itself another, contrary identity.
Who am I, apart from what others assume? A deformed
person appears banished from sex by their own body,
into the solitude of knowing that being beautiful
can be studied like a distant, dying star. Remember
those soft-porn images of lace and curves? I was sure

such skin would touch this skin, but never sure
exactly how. That was a time unaware of identity –
awash in the thrill and vertigo, I became a member
of that boy's club I couldn't belong to (I was deformed).
I held in my flesh a pre-used sense of what beautiful
meant, some detached assessment of another body.

What else to do but accept, like death, this body?
So far from desirable, I might surface on the other shore
where the soft fall of light on skin is what's beautiful –
a way of seeing, not what's seen. A stigmatised identity
can fuel anyone's resentment. Why say *deformed*
or *crippled*, when there's *striking* or even *sexy*? Remember

who keeps slamming doors in your face, remember
the nauseating, clinical chill of those rooms – each body
shaved, veiled with cosmetics, or cut and deformed
by surgeons, for *beauty*. Can anyone be sure
breaking their way in will change anything? An identity
like this might make me a fetish, but not *beautiful*.

I've only heard it spoken in whispers – *beautiful* –
by other exiles. Such tenderness is harder to remember
than cruelty, feels more frail than any given identity.
Both words and electricity surge through the body –
concepts and their fractures – so even you're unsure
what might spill out. That's why this poem is formed

around words like *beautiful* – they're more deformed
than any of us, whatever we remember. So, sure,
what I remember might be flawed, but not my body.

Prescriptions

Are words like these stimulants or anaesthetics?
Where there is no struggle, there is no strength.

You can't feel that from the stale cell of your bed.
I don't, as another load is thrown onto my back.

Where is there *no struggle*? Is there no strength
in succumbing, in the collapse? Do we have to fight?

I don't – as another load is thrown onto my back,
whether insult or pity – welcome that weight.

In succumbing, in the collapse, do we have to fight
the impulse to fight? Being different is exhausting.

Whether insult or pity, welcome that weight,
I keep telling myself, as if repeating makes it true.

The impulse to fight being different is exhausting.
Be feeble. Be ignorant. Lose. This is what

I keep telling myself. As if repeating makes it true,
experts prescribe affirmations, courage. Instead, I'll

be feeble. Be ignorant. Lose. This is what
flesh and bone want – to hold, to dissolve. Still,

experts prescribe affirmations, courage. Instead, I'll
think, *where is bird song, where is human touch?*

Flesh and bone want to hold, to dissolve. Still,
you can't feel that. From the stale cell of your bed,

think – *here is bird song, here is human touch.*
Are words like these stimulants or anaesthetics?

Crucifixion

after Francis Bacon's 1965 triptych

recognise the image   beneath   d isfiguremen t sculpted
before it registers –   the tree   from brushstroke
me   small bundle
reduced to meat   of innards and   a red not of blood
and spectacle   slick feathers   but the passions
the hook tucked inside   – the half-   twitching, mortal
this body   digested   black stuffed into cavities
          thrown-up   white skull, white bandages
genetic experiment   fledgling   tenderness of pinks
di s played   the cat found   floor of dirt, bread, dust
unnatural curve of muscle   and couldn't
organs merged   keep down   it is not finished
through an   here you are still
order or disorder   raised surgically
          light catches   nailed to an image
something you'll   in the wet   the officers have seen enough
in terro gate   flesh   for now
or get used to   sparks
          in my gut   (human most human
the others, already taken out   when barely recognisable)

we don't know but it appears   the third day
they're so aware of what is   that night   will never come
going to happen to them   scrupulous   you're stuck
they do everything to escape   she licks   with this bulk
          the back   fixed
(sometimes we don't)   of my hand   with a look

After being examined again

that's enough now
I've had   if there is
standing in front of mirrors   only here there is
breathing in and holding   the way skin breathes
lift that leg   thoughtless
wait here and read this   I would
questionless   bury my head in air
(dare I say it) for us
everyone (else) an expert   there's no need
for signs
that's enough   thought
seriously   weighs on us from the inside
forty five years
medicalised   shame
wrong   each appearance another layer
I   can't   tell   you
heart a fist
what pushes me   seed or ceding
onto the ceiling   decay
to watch   and mulch
if I   if there is
could be unre mar kable   anything but being
something burnt on
tested   the memory
under machines   let me be
not yet enough   enough
not quite here

brought   this territory six feet high
            to a small point   and infinitely
a meeting of axes   defect ive
                        in the cavity of the chest
                                                                  I would bury
                        pleas   these feet   in earth
                                                   know I’m unkn own
            these   ruins to be
                        failures   tenderly sketched or
what gift   held
                                                   so me one

Human Looking

Human looking

Mütter Museum Historic Medical Photographs, 1860–1940

> So much can go wrong. Ulcers or lesions.
> An infestation of worms. Measles, pneumonia, gangrene.
> Some unidentifiable congenital flaw.

Notice how the cursive of this young man's spine
echoes the photographer's signature. This specimen
was acquired in 1877 at a cost of fifty dollars,
on condition that *no questions were to be asked that might*
lead to its identification. I think about the word *its*.
Through this contract, he became the world's
second-tallest skeleton on display.
We are curious.   So much can go wrong.

> Sudden, multiple sarcomas. *Hysterical*
> *inability to stand or walk. Vestigial tail.*
> A body can be monstrous, shy, mercurial.

This child's head is cradled by adult hands.
It is difficult to discern whether this is for a sense
of scale, the grip tender and subtle,
or if he had to be held down for the image
to be clear enough. I also need
the inscription – *Supernumerary auricle. Idiot.*
Incontinence of urine – to believe there's anything wrong
with him. So, I look again.   So much

can go wrong. Unstable
and fatigued, I am liable to fall
into the belief that I'm not inside these photographs.

R's hair is slick and neatly combed,
crutches resting against the wall behind him.
He is dressed only in a shirt and vest, pinstripe trousers
folded so as to modestly cover his groin.
I am meant to pay attention to the stump
of his amputated right leg –   the pinched flesh
where the stitches were, hand resting in the vacated space.
It's okay, he's looking into the distance, not the camera.

How are we meant to look
at all these injuries sustained from war, from motor vehicles,
or from carrying wealthy men around on sedan chairs?

And A's body is still here –
naked and uncannily thin, bones loosely arranged
on an unmade bed. The hard facts
of his ribs and collarbone press up against his skin,
against my eyes. Surely he must be
sleeping, nestled in oblivion. Yet why
is his bedsheet pulled back to expose him
to the flinches and caresses of my gaze? So

much can go wrong. Sometimes I might think
I recognise myself in a patient,
as if their dignity or torment was mine.

In this photo of a nameless man
with an unspecified disorder of the jaw,
he looks like he may be singing.
Dressed in a tailored three-piece suit and tie,
his expression is composed, almost bored,
yet his mouth is an ecstatic, crooked *O*.
No matter how hard I strain,
I can’t hear him.

Light which acts as a mask

for the model in Joel Peter Witkin's 'Art Deco Lamp, New Mexico' (1986)

Alone and safe, you spread the newspaper across the table. Before you realise you've read them, certain words in an advertisement enter and possess. *Pinheads, dwarfs, giants, hunchbacks, hermaphrodites, bearded women, people with tails, horns, wings, reversed hands or feet, anyone born without arms, legs, eyes, ears, nose, lips. All people with unusually large genitals. All manner of extreme visual perversion.* You have tried not to think of yourself as perverted, monstrous or holy. Not a symbol, a weapon, raw material. But it seems the photographer needs you, or your form, if there is a difference. His work is his pilgrimage to become more loving, unselfish. The idea becomes you.

With your good hand, you have already dialled the number. The days before your appointment curve in on themselves, blur out of focus. You rehearse your own voice. One version is self-possessed, with a sarcastic wit. Another, tremulous and conflicted. A third, cool, almost oblivious. They distort around each other. Home loses the sense of itself. The windows are filmed with the city's mechanical air. An animal turns clumsily in the ceiling. Somehow you sleep and dreams clamber through your head, a fist of images, oddly comforting.

Only when you arrive and the equipment is laid out before you, do you realise that there was never any mention of what these sessions would precisely entail. On the table, a tangle of ropes and chains, rusted callipers, rotting fruit, a human skull, barbed wire, a broken clock. He prods and strokes your body with his eyes – especially the soft folds of flesh, the curved arc of your protruding spine. The mask is his suggestion. Your nakedness is yours.

Having a little difficulty breathing, he disappears behind the camera. You're not sure if he's struggling with this, or aroused. He orders you into myriad, difficult positions. It takes a long time for him to be satisfied. In the end, you've hardly said a word, and he has contorted your body into the shape of an ampersand, but connecting with what?

There is only the sound now of something being slid under your door – your sole payment, a print of the photograph. In the scoured image, your face is covered with a white globe – light which acts as a mask, through which you cannot look back at the viewer. You return it to the dark envelope, take up again your quiet life.

Cave

When the wound healed, and the patient was going about with his wrecked face uncovered, I was sometimes sensible of the embarrassment to which allusion has been made. I feared, when talking to him, to meet his eye, that inadvertently I might let the poor victim perceive what I had perceived: namely, that he was hideous –
Ward Muir, Orderly at Third London General Hospital, 1918

The park benches outside the hospital
were painted blue – code to the locals
to move along, in case a patient arrived.

The one I can't forget had been coaxed back into town
from a cave he was living in. *The woman I love*
finds me repugnant. She has a right to.

Our clinic walls were lined with prosthetic faces,
flags and posters. Not a single mirror.
He told me, *it was a sound like someone smashing*

a bottle in a bathtub, only my own skull
was the porcelain and the glass. What could I
possibly say to such a story? Three times a day,

I pushed a rubber tube down his throat
and poured in beef-tea or milk. Too often
it went in wrong – he'd choke and cough,

then nod, as if saying, *all ready again*.
And still you want to know what he looked like.
His surgeons worked from the inside out,

each layer – bone, flesh, skin – building up
the semblance of a face. They learnt much
through their many failures. As I did

when I looked into his eyes too deliberately.
The air between us, a frozen river.
I carry a shard of it in my stomach.

Some of the patients formed a football team.
We're guaranteed a win – the other team
take one look at us and run the opposite direction.

You might imagine he joined them on that field,
his brokenness becoming only one among many,
and that after the fifteen operations

he filled out the pension forms as suggested,
writing *repulsive*, eventually marrying
a beautiful, gentle woman. But I was not surprised

to see him, as he left the hospital, walking
towards the limits of the town, back to the ragged,
open mouth of that cave, the peace of it.

Sisyphus, deformed, looks back over his shoulder

The hill is everywhere beyond my front door
and what I carry can never be put down.

It's hard to remember a time when this
weight was separate from my body. Aware

it's being watched, the skin grows quickly
over a burden, hardens like a myth,

but keeps its sensitivity. There's a constant
hum in my inner ear, and my nervous

system is awash with fatigue. The enduring
task is to leave the house, practise the art of

oblivion, as if that could deflect your attention.
At least it's exercise. Or rehearsal. For what,

I'm not sure. Am I lifting history? Your
thoughts of me? The hill could be the entire

human world. The hill could be my shame,
steadfast and cumbersome. Each morning,

I wake spent, begin again – scale and descend,
scale and descend, the steep face of my

appearance. Who else clambers up this
fateful inclination, assumes this otherness?

At the summit, breathless, alone, all I
can do now is take it in – the vertiginous

outlook I never asked for. I have left these
impressions in the earth. I will be followed.

In itself

for Javier Botet

not anything you can quite put your finger on
but the abandoned mansion has you
cold and transfixed

then, the long, cobwebbed corridor
flickering candlelight, unbearable
tension in the soundtrack

there is someone in the corner of the dark room

faceless, coming towards you
limbs jerking and contorted – this isn't
computer generated

taking the special effects workshop was strategic
he says, *I wanted to show them my body*
was very special, very peculiar

or, in the sickly green glow of a night-vision camera,
a form, staggering –
skin like tattered rags over long bones,
hand clutching a hammer

in another scene it crawls
out of the floor towards you, crab-like,
with a moan you hear as predatory
but is more like desperate maternal grief

no human form is frightening in itself

his childhood in and out of hospitals
trouble breathing, still
a life built out of thin air

next, from the playground, you might glimpse
this slim figure at the forest's edge –

a very tall man in a dark suit – you don't want
to go with him, but his silence
and long, outstretched arms horrify and comfort

hours under heavy make-up, sometimes
I think, I've got to stop
but then, I see the monster appearing –
it's beautiful – yes! I am
that creature
smiling from the back row as they scream

No lament

after 'Quasimodo's Lament' by Judith Beveridge

(a departure, using each line's first word)

Crazed? – only the mob in us deserves that word.
Your self, your body, calm and attentive at the rope,
will always draw out those strong and slanted notes
running across every imperfect surface. Heard

as harsh racket or pure silence, your curved and heavy
bell is as perfect as kyphosis – deformed, composed.
Your torso's an ornate cathedral, a vast sanctuary.
Outside, the cobblestones echo with myths convinced

your modest and erotic heart will always be alone.
The one who desires you, though, enters with care
into the charged field around your shape. What is this

love but a deep ringing? These bodies but their secrets?
Be quiet, then, as the deft poets approach, let
them dream of capturing you. You'll be elsewhere.

Blemished

from the Rabbinic scriptures and a Buzzfeed article

A hunched back could be a misshapen eyebrow.
Withered could also be dwarf.
Some of our problems are to do with translation.

Here, perfection and human weakness touch.
You wouldn't want to distract the people from YHWH.
Without eyebrows. Missing teeth. Nose too big.
The people will stare at you. There is nothing wrong with them.

A priest is like an X-ray physician – at far more risk
than the patient. Inspiration is too much for your body to lift.
Breasts like those of a woman. Bowlegged. Epileptic.

You're shaped into a question that confounds them.
Unmatching eyes. Crushed testicles. Blind. Lame.
You can still sweep the courtyard, and eat the holy food,
but you can never offer the sacrifices.

A rare sight at Fashion Week – you walk down the runway
and the audience cheers. This is not frightening.
All you can do is love every single part

of the body you will have for the rest of your life.
You get made up, pose, look beautiful.
Pockets of the industry are ticking your box and feeling good
about themselves. Your gait reminds some of a marionette.

Today, you are the most inspirational, viral thing.
Your face, with patches of pigment missing.
How the wheels turn beneath your hands.

People who thought they were alone
send you desperate, ecstatic messages. You know
even the fit models wear padded bras and butt pads.
Has anyone even noticed the clothes?

Then the lame will leap like deer,
        the tongues of the speechless sing for joy.

Formity

alternating lines with William Hay's 'Deformity: An Essay' (1754)

imagine a print of me in the frontispiece
        or a proliferating meme in the aether
I am indeed a perfect riddle
        the disfigured can't be figured
cannot look with proper confidence in the face of another

        you don't quite know what it's like
out of tenderness they taught me to be ashamed
        what else might explain this
awkwardness of my outward get-up and behaviour
        this dream of entering the body of another

ever conscious what an untoward subject
        does to the atmosphere in a room or a poem
I feel a reluctance in opening my mouth
        who knows what might come out or in
a deformed person should not assume borrowed feathers

        or that language can speak louder than flesh
contempt attends him like his shadow reminding him of his ill figure
        as if *to figure* was not also *to think*
when I die I care not what becomes of this carcass
        while I live let me care what becomes of you

I desire my body may be opened
        as these words are opened and never fixed

and I am a good subject of speculation for all in me is nature
    an image blurred against the retina
        the pleasure of one escaped

Song not for you

after 'Das Lied des Zwerges' ('The song of the dwarf'),
Rainer Maria Rilke

Crooked blood, stunted hands, cripple,
out of place – uncanny how small
thoughts can be, while I'm incomparable,
only a dwarf because the so-called average
person is taller. You ought
to just walk on by, but don't. Ever thought
how inflated you must look from this

height? When I walk or shop, I'm inspiring,
it seems. *Fantastic to see you getting*
out, you say, as you imagine waking
up in my body, the courage
you'd need not to kill yourself, stat.
How do you live with that?
That's me wondering back,
distractedly eating (wow!) a sandwich.

In my home, I've made it so I come
face to face with the cupboards and oven, belonging
as we all want it. I sleep in my bed (some-
times alone). At work, my cubicle's longer
and wider than yours. True,
this isn't much of a song –
but then it never was meant for you.

Not a performance

Mike Parr, 'Foreign Looking' (National Gallery of Australia, 2016)

I push through a thick black curtain, watch
his body opened and hurt on three walls
in films which loop and bleed into each other
unsure if it's right to call this *performance*
as his left thigh is encircled with a scalpel
a garter of blood smeared across his face
his belly flinches as lit matches land on skin
white paint poured into the mouth, vomited out
then an old wound is opened and stitched back up
that's the point I turn away to read the list of films –
        no, there's no indication how long this will last

I want to believe a body suffering alone
is an impossibility, this flickering in the bowels
another deep empathic contraction, so that
even here, in the adjoining forest of bronze heads
which glance at a wall of thoughtful self-portraits –
smudged charcoal, scribbled skin, frail canvas –
my inner ears prickle with sound from the other rooms
anthemic song, foreboding static, wincing and groans
finally the awkward applause recorded in the gallery
audience wrenching themselves back to the safety of art
        afraid the unspeakable cannot be contained

in 1950s Lismore, the other kids would ask
what happened to his arm, nothing below the elbow
casually, he'd blow a hole in reality, say *oh it*
got caught in the chaff cutter and fed to the cows
language begins and ends here in that empty space
where his hand would be, each wound
an exclamation mark in search of a sentence
after trauma, he says, *I can think*
but there is another kind of pain – enclosed
in a sweltering room, the future amputated,
          even a thought becomes torture

in *Close the Concentration Camps*, the word
alien branded on his thigh, on a hardback chair
in the centre of the gallery, he has his lips,
ears, face sewn into a web of bloodied thread
mostly, we stand at a distance, backs to the wall
no way to look at him without seeing ourselves
reflected back in a mirror – distressing
the smell of burnt flesh and antiseptic
what could this mean? what is happening
here and in those failing places, which
          fourteen years on are even further away?

*   *   *

removed from ████████ themselves
these are bodies ████████████
████████████ not ████
██████████████ safe ███
████████████ what is human ████
██████ food, ███ detergent, ███
█ a blade ████████ an anchor point
somehow these cries and silences leak out
through the heavy curtain of distance and law
as if pulled in by the empty space inside our bodies
which shivers, resounds with that pain

Unrecognised

National Portrait Gallery, Canberra

At five, the doors click shut. Security
walks a final circuit and clocks off. The eyes
of the prominent are lost in the middle distance

beyond office, sports field or studio. Hair and skin
of oil, watercolour, polymer, the reassurance
of names everyone should know. Not ours –

we are without shelter, without conservation.
But they cannot keep us out. At dusk,
white walls become grey, darken.

When it's safe, someone gives the signal.
From the coal-black cloakroom chiming
with empty hangers, through a broken

shutter at the gift shop, from underneath
the doors of an out-of-service toilet, we emerge,
move through the gallery as smoke

or pheromones. In the dim cool,
minute cracks in the canvas, paper, plaster,
open like pores to breathe us in.

Morning, the first visitor examines
each portrait, as if trying to remember
or forget. Something about that black scar

of paint, the dishevelled bed in the background,
soft fold of belly flesh, or the polished glass
    from which his own face gazes back.

Impression

Each night, when I'm prone, the
ceiling watches me. By
day, the walls, or clouds and
you. I'm wrapped in sober
clothes, in skin, in words that
come from others' mouths.
Misshapen, I can't lie
straight in bed. Upright, I'm
not. Up close, of course, the
surface blurs and whispers.
There's neck-pulse, wrist-pulse, a
soft knocking at my ribs
from the inside. I'm not
empty. There are sparks and
ashes, microplastics
and trace metals, pollen,
stone, unfinished love. Some
of that spills out. I pace
the grey corridors of
my head. But you might know
me from the footpaths and
gardens of the real world.
When I walk, I'm part-
giraffe, part-heron, all
this, whoever this is.
I can't sit still. Chairs tend
to cripple, repel. At

least this means I'm leaning
forward, towards you. A
curious parenthesis
of bone and open pores.
But yes, ordinary,
moving, I displace air
much like you do. And in
the bed, the couch, I can
see the imprint of my
shape. I am held here.

Change Room

Hephaestus

My first memory is falling,
the look of disgust on my father's face.

Even the air I hurtled through was desperate
to be relieved of me. My body, broken

as I broke through the surface of the ocean
that accepted me. I had to stay within

its cold depths to learn anything.
They know me as the lame, pitiful one.

But here I am standing among the other
gods with a hammer in my soft hand, never

quite knowing what to do with this
strange material, this avalanche of fire falling

endlessly within me. Now and then,
an Olympian subcontractor comes unannounced

to break my legs again, or to add a deforming
trace of arsenic to the metal.

They need to keep me at the forge,
shaping their breastplates and their helmets

from something formless. They need me
continually in some stage of recovery.

My callipers are made of gold and fractured,
repurposed lines. I'm not the god of poetry,

but of sculpture and volcanoes. I've tried
to disappear into the sudden closing sunset,

the glistening carapace of the beetle, the dark
red warmth of the earth. But I know

where I belong, and that walking –
getting anywhere – is a kind of falling.

The change room

This morning, walking almost naked
from the change room towards the outdoor heated pool,
I become *that man* again, unsettling

shape to be explained.
Such questions aren't asked to my face. Children
don't mean anything by it, supposedly, so I

shouldn't feel as I do,
as my bones crouch into an old shame I thought
I'd left behind. Chlorine prickling

my nostrils, a stranger
compliments me on my tattoos and shows me hers –
a dove in flight over a green peace sign –

as if the canvas was unremarkable.
She turns and limps away,
and something makes a moment of sense.

I lower myself into our element
and swim, naturally
asymmetrical and buoyant. Quite some time

later, showering, the man beside me
is keen to chat – how many laps we've each done,
how long I've lived in this town, the deep

need for movement.
Speaking, our bodies become solid.

Mutual obligation

the institutions hollowed out, you're cornered by an idea of
independence rent-stress and diagnosis
work, the only rope thrown into the hole

some of those employed do well, seem intact, while others are rushed
to emergency, missing a limb or a mind
left with the therapy of paperwork

your body employs you in the labour of bone-pain and flesh-hurt
the small steps through the pharmaceutical minefield
the work of falling to earth

the tenure of trying to do no harm to yourself, the painstaking
translations of the body's murmurs and sparks
the work of being human

on call to climb precarious impairment tables, to prove just how
incapable you are, and yet how able and willing
you do want to work don't you?

still this hacking through forests of symptoms and prescriptions,
desperate to lie down in a sunlit clearing, to rest
to be heard and to be held

in the mutual obligation of shared air, where the work consists of
listening to each other's troubled breathing
with no solution to offer but this

Reduced

Turning, disturbed, from your confession
to read your reduced sentence, we'll understand

your exhaustion, cornered and bereft,
having already lost the child you'd hoped for.

You gave up pleading with the department,
the doctors, the school, your partner, your god.

The weight of him, larger every day
on your shoulders. You just wanted sleep,

some respite, the one you dreamed would come.
A child who'd learn to dress and clean himself,

say *I love you* in some kind of language,
something, anything, behind his eyes.

When they found him, he was unrecognisable.
You were there too – the curtains drawn,

the television on, the room full of static.
They couldn't get a word out of you.

Instructions for client restraint

to minimise disruption for others and in order for us to get
anything done around here sometimes it has to be cobbled
together with wooden planks and chicken wire you
can't call it a cage it's more a withdrawal space with
padlocks on the outside and a warning this report contains

bruises can't say
what happened restraint
marks on the wrists and
ankles for their own good
strapped into a chair or
bed or toilet seat unable
to consent or speak who
would believe her anyway
the work may attract a few bad
apples access to vulnerable
non-verbal or immobile
people either way how to
make a complaint against
the person who cleans
you clothes you is
there while you sleep

unreliable testimony
difficult behaviours
moaning complex needs
no other options codes of
practice expert care these
burdens are tragic this
construction a space where
he might quieten down or
scream into exhaustion
or maybe try extra medi-
cation adrenal fatigue
low pay high turnover
lack of training no doubt
it can be distressing for
family members to hear
about every single incident

a pacified body is a pacified mind a space of restraint
creates a strange peacefulness at the centre as if there is
no one there as the funding evaporates or is siphoned off
disability always is other people the oversight challenged
a report is made and filed again it won't be accessible

The way of uselessness

The source of all things made a mess
of Crippled Tree – crooked back,
organs bunched up, chin at his belly.
I'm at peace, he said, with the violence
of the seasons. If my right arm
becomes a rooster, I can keep watch.
If my arse becomes wheels,
I'll never need a carriage.

Crippled No-Lips and Swollen-Neck
both spoke eloquently to the Duke
and soon enough he found the bodies
of normal people repulsive.
Knowledge is a curse.
Form, without form.

A chestnut tree observed
how the hawthorn, pear and orange
were cruelly treated for being useful.
So it made its wood brittle, seeped sap
from its side, disguised itself as a shrine.
It grew old and huge,
became shade for thousands of oxen.

Young Horse-Face had no official position,
didn't know anything,
not even his own ugliness.

The Cultural Revolution broke my spine.
Students took me to a secret room.
For months, they show me their fists,
distort my body with hunger, demand
I confess. But there is nothing to confess.
When one of them turns away,
I push myself out a window,
plunge three storeys into uselessness.

This was the era when the doorsteps
of the orphanages were crowded.
No boys – only girls and the useless ones.
Each week they decide who can be fed
and who will be placed, without a name,
into the other rooms.

Years later, my sister finds me
alone in the shelter, the walls, my arms,
stained with dried shit –
I want to follow her tears back to our home
but what will happen
to the others? The source of all things
rests heavily on my shoulders.

Twenty-five years later, I can say –
too many problems but big achievements.
The road ahead is very long –

Yet all men wanted to learn from him,
women to be his concubines.
He was given the reins of government
and immediately he left
to go rambling through the forest
unknown.

Zhuang Zhou,Taoist sage,
fourth century BCE

unstable, with many potholes –
so it is not a question of character
but of surfaces. Through my window, I see
a woman, burnt in an industrial accident,
turned away again. This is just
an administrative centre, not a service facility.

Deng Pufang, one of the founders of the
Chinese Disabled Persons' Federation, b.1944

Becoming

from memory and a Hocąk tale

some futile thing that can't be secured
(attention or a plastic toy – does it matter?)
he slams his bedroom door
stands for a long moment before
the goldfish bowl
and knocks (a part of him,
split off, will call it an accident, knowing it wasn't)
the food container
into the water – their small happy mouths
open and open
(greedily we fill ourselves with regret)
the fish float on the surface
suddenly he finds it hard to breathe

two men go out hunting
their quarry (a racoon, or a spirit in disguise)
disappears into the hollow
of an immense tree and they find there
a fish
one plucks it out and cooks it
offers morsels to the other, who isn't sure
but wanting what his friend has, he takes and eats
immediately becoming
unbearably thirsty
he drinks but no water is enough
frantic, he wades out into the river
scales cover his skin, gills open in his neck

Reading deformity

Khujjuttarā was hunchbacked.
In a previous life she saw a holy man,
one who was enlightened only for himself.

He walked across her path, his back slightly stooped.
She threw a blanket over her shoulder,
bent over and imitated his way of moving.

The translation somehow made me think this
was an act of solidarity. Becoming
crippled. Much like bone, my thoughts

shape themselves, even after re-reading that
in fact she had mocked him, was made deformed
to turn her from wrong thinking, wrong behaviour.

Empathy began in the early twentieth century,
adapted from the German for *feeling into.*
An expectant mother is frightened at the sight

of an elephant, or thinks too intensely
about strawberries, a burning house
or an execution. In the womb, we make ourselves

deformed through empathy. Involuntary contractions
of certain muscles in the mind. You read this
and who knows what shape your body takes on.

Survival

A landscape of exposed bone, taut muscle. Sky –
as white as it is blue. Hard light
pushing through shadows of lace.

Each morning, whether in drought or frost,
the town wakes to the sound
of something shifting under the surface.

The fields are pocked with hand-dug shafts.
Miners with no lamplight or luck
walked and fell into their graves.

Most of the topsoil, washed away in the hungry rush.
Now, whatever grows here, grows strong
and broken.

In a café, a stranger walks you through the ruins of her life.
Memories stir beneath her voice,
tremors along her arm.

These muted boulders and fallen leaves,
these cockatoos scratching the dry air,
aren't interested in healing you.

A kangaroo's paws touch the rough edge of the road,
pink X over his still warm body.
The ground absorbs all he knew.

Today, you surface in the middle of the reservoir,
face to face with the dark, inscrutable calm
of a musk duck.

Tiny heads of pink or yellow float on fine stalks. To see
these wildflowers, you have to stop,
crouch down and wait.

You still don't know a word of the language of this place.
Syllables drift on the wind,
dust-motes catch in the throat.

Inflection, across the seas

after Jane Hirshfield's 'Inflection finally ungraspable by grammar'

for J.G. and O.

Each lap of the pool is much the same.
The repetition, for me, is calming.
Showering, I find a terribly long, thin hair

has knotted itself around my right hand.

It's not that difficult to remove,
though sense-memories cling.
You, elsewhere, have woken again

under so much water, inside your own vast heart,

weighed down with the drenched clothes
of others' interrupted stories,
their indefinite grief –

and you're not sure which way the surface is,

or what difference your words make.
He has been refusing to eat for weeks.
To ebb away, the only asylum he can imagine.

Somehow, together, you reach the shore.

Without thinking, we each open our mouth
and taste whatever rushes in –
fresh bread, fathomless depths, a feeding tube.

And you, with all this in your head, what can you do?

They have excised every island,
turned back every boat,
buried their hands in the water of themselves.

Clear air

for the residents of Tsukui Lily Garden, Sagamihara, Japan

breaking a window   I bring clear air
                                        into the wards

thinking of my tired country
the economy weighed down

night shift   only six workers
                    to tie up   I apologise to them

                                        new moon   the sound
of my footsteps   as I move from room to

the neck a more merciful
                    place   than the chest to open

                                        eight homes in the facility –
dream   flower   rainbow   the pleiades   breath   harvest

something stops me entering *wings   hope*
          where I used to work   with these people

                                        one of the knife handles
hurts a little   after a while   I must use another

security cameras blink
          I walk across the screen   no one watching

tweet *I hope for world peace*
beautiful Japan!   many likes comments retweets

I turn myself in   the officers seem unsurprised
but the blood

I plead not guilty by reason of insanity   I will
be *taken care of*   each night I watch the news   the tv in
a cage on the wall   shows a photo of my face   then soon
enough gone   no honour or dishonour   as if nothing has
happened

each new moon   the sound
of footsteps outside my room   that never arrive

Burdens

Forgetting the extermination is part of the extermination itself

Jean Baudrillard

Great care must be taken to record the cause
as consistent with the patient's prior condition.
Family members still love these creatures. Therefore
the smallest mistake is likely to arouse suspicion.

'Pneumonia' is an ideal cause of death for our action,
since it is widely considered such a critical illness.
Simply calculate a longer decline for the young.
Relatives like to believe in an end that is painless,

therefore 'a stroke' is ideal for the older patients.
Write to them advising that in this time of war
incineration of their remains was essential
and their possessions were distributed to the poor.

What we are engaged in is irreproachable.
Though we must ensure it is as secret as possible.

/

the only explanation I can give is that I didn't have enough time to think
about it all the nurses were put under a lot of stress

please believe me I didn't do it readily I really detested it in fact I can't
say why I didn't refuse

at that time there wasn't anybody to pour out one's heart to nobody
would have helped us if we refused to do the work

you don't have the level of education of a physician you can't evaluate
if the order is right one's own thinking is switched off

at the time I thought I wouldn't be guilty if I didn't do the actual killings
I tried to cope with it as far as possible to forget everything

you ask me if I would also have committed a theft on order I say that I
wouldn't have done it however I saw the act of giving medicine
even in order to kill as an obligation

my attitude was if it was me I would consider it a release

/

beer, wine and cocktails
a local polka band
all the hospital staff
crammed into the basement
one of the doctors
gives an inspiring, sober speech on the importance of our work
more beer, laughter
the administrator dressed as a priest
delivers a mock eulogy
applause as the ten-thousandth patient
is pushed into the furnace
more wine, dancing
you and I
stagger through the Hadamar facility gardens, singing

/

Our institution, and many others, obtained
wonderful research material. I gave the officers
the jars, the fixatives and instructions,
          that's all. The advancement of science

requires a constant supply.   I know now
that some of the younger physicians – aware
of the various bonuses, research grants
and university appointments on offer –

took it on themselves to 'take up a collection'
from the smaller hospitals and clinics – those with
harelips, stutters, cerebral palsy, feeble-mindedness,

                    any noticeable deformities at all.
They are still teaching us about ourselves –
          ironic, given their abnormality.

/

Q1.
The construction of a lunatic asylum costs six million marks. How many houses at 15,000 marks each could have been built for that amount?

Q2.
A handicapped person costs the public five Reichsmarks per day. If within the boundaries of the Reich 300,000 of

these people are being cared for in institutions, how many marriage loans at 1,000 Reichsmarks per couple could be financed annually from the funds allocated to institutions?

Q3.
This person suffering from hereditary defects costs the people 60,000 Reichsmarks during his lifetime. If a loaf of bread costs 0.63 Reichsmarks, how many loaves could be supplied for that amount?

/

First, let me be
clear, everything in medicine and ethics is relative.
Each part of the body serves the whole. The people,
the nation. Wherever there exists a terrible burden, it is right
to remove it. Let's be honest now. Human
husks. Disgusting travesties. Useless eaters.
Where there is no suffering, there can be no pity.
Any normal person would be appalled to imagine
themselves in such a state. The economy,
the state. Burdens. What will happen to us
if we do not act to disinfect? The body, the society,
the diagnosis. These people, these –

/

why write this now?

at the time (of course)

one knew

smoke over the town
                    ash in the river

one found oneself unsettled
                    distracted   un-   dis-

the children would taunt each other
                    with the name of the hospital

day after day they arrived
                    grey buses with darkened windows

I wrote a number of strongly worded letters

why write this now?
                    who does it benefit?

Warm and Dark

Dedication

Narrative of the Life of James Allen, the Highwayman, Being His Death-bed Confession, 1837

You hold what remains of his life
in your white-gloved hands. The heft

of the book leaves an imprint on your palms.
Such thin, fragile leaves –

hard to believe the weight of them.
Or how they have been held together.

A solid, tender thing, bound with a familiar
material. *Aristocratic leather*

was one euphemism. The body, flayed.
The skin, dried and tanned. Beside

a creeping realisation, you find yourself
admiring the aesthetic rigour –

how the raw materials of a book
can amplify its content. This flawed,

hardened skin once held an entire life.
Inside, a highwayman lays bare the intimate

details of his career of violence. His final wish –
that it be made into the bindings

of this book you now hold. The dedication
seems sincere – to the only man

who bravely refused to surrender up his possessions,
please accept this final gift – as if this cover,

when touched, could touch back.

Warm and dark

What has happened to me? he thought. It was no dream.

Franz Kafka, *The Metamorphosis*

You wake to the sensation of
something solid and barely alive
inside you. Tiny, pointed
        feet upon your tongue,
thread-antennae brushing your palate,
it has made its way over
the soft threshold of lips for a place
        to rest or die. Half-asleep, you

reach in, grasp and toss
the slick, leathery presence across
the bedroom, switch the light on,
        needing but not wanting to know
what you already suspect.
You gargle, twice, but it persists
as a ghost in your mouth.
        The next day, one secretes itself

into a nook under the toaster,
spreading an uncanny electric smell
through the house as it dies. Another
        hides between the wall and that pile
of anthologies, scuttling away as you reach
for the stillness of words. At night,
you remember reading how
        the cockroach can't walk backwards –

so in a confined space, such as the ear canal,
they can only burrow further in
with their mouthparts, finding
        escape and sustenance at once.
And you can't find sleep – only
the thought of them moving through
shadows, searching for somewhere
        warm and dark.

Microbiome

While we live, we ourselves are inhabited
William Bryant Logan, *Dirt: The Ecstatic Skin of the Earth*

In the earth, prepared and silent, what will I
be offering you? It's said the menu opens

with the liver and the brain, for their wealth
of enzymes and water, the heart
before the bones. But so many of you

are already here at this soft table, always hungry,
unfussy. I've been feeding you protein,

fibre, starch, sugar, paper and ink,
self-consciousness, the crimson jolt of the rosella
in the leafless tree, my own dying cells,

hesitation in the face of violence, more water,
the scent of the skin of the one I love,

confusion with almost everything else.
And what will you make of all this
turning? Warm compost, what remains.

There are many pleasures

the first has your mouth flush with milk taste of clear
blue sky sounds of soft fur sweet smell of sun and shadow
in a blur of senses gently vexing everything rushing in
was that how it was back then before you could hold
words or make memory these pleasures (making you)

others you soon realise are built from detritus and thin air
your first bike and a vacant lot of roller-coaster dirt paths
pocket-money shrapnel swapped for a bag of mixed sugars
blue bruises twisted ankles accidental scars compelling
as they're absorbed slowly into the flesh (alchemical)

but what version of it makes you the only one not laughing
your marrow registering that acid attention before you do
a joke a shove a name to become punchline and exile but
pinned there and kept as someone else's strange pleasure
the little needles of that sound still inside you (as ballast)

this one is timid and hides when you take out your pen
but unwatched it'll sneak into the ink or disguise itself
as the seeds of tears or kisses the soft percussion of rain
your breath fizzing feather-soft through mirror-neurons
as thought grows tired and unclenches (a hinge creaks)

then there's her wise palm tender on your cheek
that crack in your frost would be pleasure enough
but to see something pure welling up from the centre
of her chest to know she has surfaced through fathomless
pain into herself this frail and fierce light (

Opening the urn

Your last sound, as you clutched your chest
and fell onto the winter-chilled grass,
was a bewildered, involuntary
oh –
I know you
preferred the consonants. So much
of what you knew, you kept locked up,
disavoweled. And here,
in the hospital, the ventilator is your body's
ventriloquist. This rendition
of our simplest human song is unconvincing.
There are tears in me
that won't budge.

+

My brother and I enter through the unlocked
back door. It reminds me, Mum,
of coming home after school, hungry,
while you were still at work.
Except this time,
the lounge room is already warm, on the stove
is a stew for one, a few boiled vegetables,
and we've just told the hospital
they can turn the machines off. You thought,
of course, you'd return. My brother,
famished, eats from the saucepan.

+

Back home, in my own pale bathroom,
the orchid flowers
are opening their sweet, flushed mouths.
Their chorus resounds in my chest
like a curse.   An ant of want,
insect of grief, I am failing
to find any scent path, but stagger
over the lip
into your absence.

+

At the doorway to what was
your bedroom, now crammed with boxes
the Salvos will pick up – meaningless
crockery, tupperware, too many towels –
I only pause   for a moment
to breathe the disappearing air,
(if I leave this house now
it will be like pushing your coffin into the furnace again)
and something hungry
under the floorboards has my bones
forgetting how to hold me up –
my crumpled keening,
you'd be embarrassed by it.

+

    Slicing through your name with the dull blade
of a pair of your scissors, I hope
underneath this pragmatic label I'll find
a way to open this urn
to let you out.   You have become subtle,
broken up into memory, smoke and ash.
I imagine – only imagine –
    slipping with the effort, my hand
                a cup of blood.

Home

Unnoticed, something in the cartilage
of the house begins to deteriorate.

Years of drought crumble the earth,
shift the bones. Home is an ageing body

that seems to cause no trouble. Each night
I sleep through it. A fine mist of plaster

dusts the bedhead, tiny grey-white pebbles
halo the furniture. A crack slowly opens

along the ceiling edge – one night, filament-thin,
the next, finger-width. Cold, dark air breathes

down towards me. 3 a.m. The long bulk
of the cornice stirs, begins to detach. From above,

a rasping, tearing – something gives way,
low rumble becoming thunder, crashing

through oblivion into muscle and core –
like prey, the body moves before thought.

The collapse, waiting, patient in the roof-space,
has plunged the room into a cloud

of debris, plaster shards, dust, the remains of insects.
And I am standing in the doorway, white-faced,

looking back at the bed, the fallen broken
cornice, where my body is not.

Lines from an ECG

for Norman Jackson (1926–1973)

the heart is not a precision instrument –
                                listen, now, it seems to stop and
start and stop and start, as if ambivalent –
                                no metronome but a poem of muscle

with an iambic limping – I am, I am
                                almost the age you were when yours
failed and you fell from a hospital bed
                                into the unsaid – *diastole* and *systole*,

how these chambers fill with blood and
                                love, then urgently send them back out –
the heart's door, always swinging on
                                its hinges – surely the aorta must tire

of this back and forth, contract, relax, old
                                unsolvable argument of flesh – between
each beat, a tiny pause, spark that will
                                one day expand to fill the whole

body – the problem, not any imperfection
                                in its rhythm, but how too much pressure
can open a tear in the wall – yes, I must
                                get checked, each year, each year –

now as the ECG turns my insistent meter
into sound, I hear whale song sped-up,
then the slow-motion crack of a whip –
the cold silence underneath –

Flesh

for R.

it feels meaningful but isn't   the ornamental plums
dropped   crushed   at the feet of their trees

cockatoos want the stone not the flesh   there isn't
anywhere clear to stand   it's all a mess only the ants

and the earth will accept   how have you managed
to cross the churning cold strait   with that fresh hollow

torn into your body   already your mother's
jumper is losing her scent   a snippet of her hair

curled into a box   you could say we're both
at home now   but we own nothing   and death

has eaten holes into our clothes   the flywire   our skin
the backyard a carpet of bitter debris   and I want you

more than ever   and the world is all flesh

Under the study

slowly realising
it's not a broken pipe

the wincing smell
        too familiar

your house on a gradual hill
something

has crawled into the vertex
        out of reach

what rises from underneath
                ghostly

        if a ghost were flesh
                deconstructing itself

more microbial cells in you than human

it's only a matter of time
                the plumber says

you keep the door shut
but the phone rings
                from inside the room

there are poems to print
and each day curiosity
          itching at the cavities of you

body without identity
                    dispersing into

Distance

McCraith House, Dromana

we drive past a fake hotel, the freeway's public art
but the distance and this posture I'm in finds me a long way
from post-modern – something in my hip ratchets up
beyond distracting into pain, thickening a fog in my head
so that you, right beside me, seem further away – yet when

we arrive and climb the steep steps to the first floor
these wall-high windows let me breathe in the entire sky –

swathes of light the clouds concede drift across the bay
and from the perspective of canopy, this glimpse of a way
of seeing beyond human time or decay, blue-green calm
broken by the merest whiteness of wave-peaks, the familiar
city on the horizon obscured in mist – and suddenly

a brilliant intelligence lands there in the bird bath – so close –
wet feathers turning his form into a personhood of wings,

delicate feet, thirst and pleasure, head a-swivel, cautiously joyful
then gone – and we're here, your eyes reflected in mine,
a reminder of what can disappear into the undergrowth
of bodies under stress, but is still there, deep in the molecules,
warm and dormant – I carry it, ignorant, and it carries me, out

through the huge window into this precious, frightening distance –
we grow older together and love, this love, burrows further in –

There was no consolation

nothing that could be held
in the mind or the hand.
The shallow

leaf-washed creek flowed on.
The steep gorge-side
held thin eucalypts and fallen

boulders. The sun
was everywhere. Around us,
blue wrens hopped, almost

into our open hands.
You brushed my arm, casually,
tenderly. A strong wind

picked up and did not
take any of this away.
Still, the pain

dug further in, muttering
in a language I could
not comprehend –

And the birds, the birds
kept feasting on insects
too small to see.

When a line of determined ants carries away my nail clippings

I remember this pale skin will be taken by the sky
my knees are already dedicated to the cracked earth

lungs, possessed by the ghost gums along the railway line
my inner ear, by shivers and nothingness

these feet belong to some restless, prayerful abstraction
language waits to inherit my expressive fingers

shares in my larynx are held by everyone I love
my blood, though, is anyone's

cloud-drift, mould-bloom, worm-hole, the waxing moon,
the cat's sensitive chin – all hold interests in this flesh

my leaning tower of vertebrae can go to the highest bidder
these tear ducts, to the lowest

sometimes it seems lost property holds my tongue
but who owns these elbows? this nose? these lymph nodes?

valves and tissues will be given to people waiting patiently in a line
my chest cavity has given itself to the song of shy birds

and these eyes, to the claim of your eyes

Notes

'Operations' is constructed from text from my own childhood medical file.

'Venus with BIID' is indebted to 'Do No Harm: Why Do Some People Want to Cut Off a Perfectly Healthy Limb?' by Anil Ananthaswamy (*Matter*, 14 November 2012); 'Amputees by Choice: Body Integrity Identity Disorder and the Ethics of Amputation' by Tim Bayne and Neil Levy (*Journal of Applied Philosophy*, vol. 22.1, 2005); 'Interrogating Transability: A Catalyst to View Disability as Body Art' by Bethany Stevens (*Disability Studies Quarterly*, vol. 31.4, 2011); and the website *The Wheelchair Zone: Where Wheelchair Users and BIID/Transabled Unite*.

Every second line in 'Unhomely' is taken from 'The Handicapped' by Randolph Bourne (*Atlantic Monthly*, September 1911).

'Borne Away by Distance' is an erasure poem, with the final chapter of *Frankenstein* by Mary Shelley (1818) as the source text.

'Pillow Angel' was written in response to the *Pillow Angel* website, and 'Forever Small: The Strange Case of Ashley X' by Eva Feder Kittay (*Hypatia*, vol. 26.3, 2011).

'Prescriptions' was written in response to a prompt provided by Jess Fairfax for *Cafe Philosophique Des Toilette*, a spoken word and philosophy event inspired by public toilet graffiti (Alex Theatre, St Kilda, 24 March 2018).

'Human looking' responds to images in *Mütter Museum: Historical Medical Photographs*, ed. Gretchen Worden (2002).

'Light which acts as a mask' speaks back to Joel-Peter Witkin's photograph 'Art Deco Lamp, New Mexico' (1986).

'Cave' is a documentary poem, composed from multiple stories of WWI soldiers. It includes phrases from Ward Muir's *Observations of an Orderly* (1917).

'In itself' is a biographical poem for the actor Javier Botet, who has the same genetic condition I have, Marfan Syndrome. It draws from 'How Javier Botet's Unique Look Launched His Career Playing Scary Monsters' by Rebecca Ford (*The Hollywood Reporter*, 20 July 2017) and 'Javier Botet: Could the 6'7", 120 Pounds Actor Be Horror's Saviour? (*The Independent*, 2 March 2016).

'No Lament' is a respectful reply to Judith Beveridge's poem 'Quasimodo's Lament' (*Meanjin*, Winter 2017).

'Blemished' includes text from 'This Model with Vitiligo is Possibly the Most Inspirational Thing You'll See Today' by Kimberley Dadds (*Buzzfeed*, 2 May 2014); 'Model Danielle Sheypuk: "People With Disabilities Are Consumers of Fashion"' by Ruth Spencer (*The Guardian*, 31 December 2016); 'These Models with Disabilities Featured in an Inspiring New York Fashion Show' by Rossalyn Warren (*Buzzfeed*, 17 February 2016); and *The Perfect Priest* by Jared Wilson (George Fox University Masters Thesis, 2013).

Every second line in 'Formity' is taken from 'Deformity: An Essay' by William Hay (1754).

'Song not for you' is a riposte to 'Song of the Dwarf' by Rainer Maria Rilke (1902, translation by Robert Bly in 1977).

'Reduced' loosely responds to some of the accounts of the parents of disabled children in *Far From the Tree* by Andrew Solomon (2014).

'Instructions for client restraint' includes accounts found in the Senate Community Affairs Reference Committee Report from 2015, *Violence, Abuse and Neglect Against People with Disability in Institutional and Residential Settings*. The poem was written before the beginning of the Royal Commission into Violence, Abuse, Neglect and Exploitation of People with Disability, which is ongoing. May it finally result in radical systemic change.

'The way of uselessness' is a response to *The Essential Chuang Tzu*, by Sam Hamill and Jerome P. Seaton (1999); 'Authorizing a Disability Agency in Post-Mao China: Deng Pufang's Story as Biomythography' by Matthew Kohrman (*Cultural Anthropology*, vol. 18.1, 2003); and 'Crippling Injustice' by James Palmer (*Aeon*, 17 February 2014).

'Becoming' includes a reference to a non-private Hocąk story, 'The Were-Fish', found in *The Encyclopedia of Hocąk Mythology*, compiled by Richard L. Dieterle.

'Reading deformity' responds to the etymology of 'empathy' and to the story of Khujjuttarā in Buddhist Pali canon. It is also informed by 'Disability on a Different Model: Glimpses of an Asian heritage' by M. Miles (*Disability and Society*, vol. 15.4, 2000).

'Survival' was written on Dja Dja Wurrung country, in acknowledgement of First Nations sovereignty and knowledge of the land.

'Clear air' is an elegy for the nineteen disabled people killed on 26 July 2016. Thank you to the reporting and commentary of Philip Brasor ('Victims of Sagamihara Massacre at Disabled Facility Are Forever Nameless', *The Japan Times*, 6 August 2016), Carly Findlay ('The Silence

Around the Sagamihara Disability Murders', carlyfindlay.com, 28 July 2016), and Eleanor Warnock and Mitsuru Obe ('Mass Killing in Japan Shocks a Gentle Nation', *The Wall Street Journal: Asia Edition*, 26 July 2016).

'Burdens' draws from the ground-breaking account by Suzanne E. Evans, *Forgotten Crimes: The Holocaust and People with Disabilities* (2004), and is an elegy for the estimated 200,000 murdered in the T-4 and related Nazi programs.

'Dedication' refers to the edition of *Narrative of the Life of James Allen, the Highwayman, Being His Death-bed Confession, 1837* which is bound in the author's own skin.

'Flesh' is for Rachael Wenona Guy, in memory of Molly Guy and Anne Jackson.

Acknowledgements

I am acutely grateful to the editors of the following journals, newspapers and anthologies, for publishing poems from *Human Looking* in their final or earlier forms.

Australian Poetry Journal, Connotation Press, Cordite, Double Dialogues, foam:e, Foglifter, Island, Meniscus, Rabbit, Softblow, StylusLit, The Saturday Paper, Verity La: Disrupt, and *Westerly*; *Abstractions*, ed. Paul Munden & Shane Strange (Recent Work Press, 2018), *The Best Australian Poems 2016 & 2017*, ed. Sarah Holland-Batt (Black Inc), *To End All Wars*, ed. Dael Allison, Anna Couani, Kit Kelen & Les Wicks (Puncher & Wattman, 2018), *Not Quite Right For Us: Forty Writers Speak Volumes*, ed. Sharmilla Beezmohun (flipped eye, 2021).

Some poems were also shortlisted or longlisted for prizes. Profound thanks to the judges of the University of Canberra Vice-Chancellor's International Poetry Prize ('Hephaestus'), the University of Canberra Health Poetry Prize ('There was no consolation'), the Newcastle Poetry Prize ('Operations'), the ACU Prize for Poetry ('Human looking'), the Melbourne Poets Union International Poetry Competition ('Aesthetic surgery'), and the Grieve Project Writing Competition ('Flesh').

An edited version of 'Separation' was adapted by Rachael Wenona Guy and Leonie Van Eyk into a stop-motion animation film 'Secessionist', which screened as part of a theatre performance 'Each Map of Scars' at the 2017 Castlemaine State Festival. An honour to work with you.

About the author

Andy Jackson's first collection, *Among the Regulars*, was shortlisted for the 2011 Kenneth Slessor Prize for Poetry; in 2020 his collection *Music Our Bodies Can't Hold* was shortlisted for the John Bray Poetry Award. He has featured at literary events and arts festivals in Ireland, India, the USA and across Australia, and has co-edited disability-themed issues of the literary journals *Southerly* and *Australian Poetry Journal*. Andy Jackson works as a creative writing teacher and tutor for community organisations and universities.